The Bus Company The Bus Company The Bus Company The Bus Company The Bus Company

000001

Who's driving your bus?

000001

The Bus Company The Bus Company The Bus Company The Bus Company The Bus Company

ANDY GILBERT & NADINE TAYLOR

D0067405

First published in Great Britain in 2003 by
Go MAD Books
Pocket Gate Farm
Off Breakback Road
Woodhouse Eaves
Leicestershire
LE12 8RS

British Library Cataloguing in Publication Data.
A catalogue record for this book is available from the British Library.

ISBN 0-9537284-9-8

Printed and bound in Great Britain by
Cox & Wyman, Reading

About the authors

ANDY GILBERT

Andy is Group Managing Director of Go MAD Ltd, a values driven consultancy with offices in the UK, Singapore and Australia and his passion is clear... to help others understand and develop their ability to make a difference.

This unwavering passion has taken Andy around the world, to hundreds of organisations and thousands of individuals, as a coach, consultant, professional speaker and established author, to help people learn the essential skills and knowledge needed to make a difference.

It all started in 1997 when Andy led a research project to find an answer to the question:

"What is the simplest way of explaining the success process that people naturally use when making a difference?"

The 14-month research project resulted in the development of a revolutionary framework that came to be known as the Go MAD® (Make A Difference) process. Andy's ability to simplify complex concepts into easily understandable and practical tools has generated demand in the corporate arena and Andy is often called to lead cultural transformation, organisational change and leadership programmes. He has authored over 50 books, training manuals and video programmes including 'Go MAD - The Art of Making A Difference', 'Go to Work on Your Career' and 'Go MAD About Coaching'.

NADINE TAYLOR

Nadine has worked in Financial Services since 1985 and joined the HR team in 1993. Her first HR role was as a Training and Development Consultant. In 1996 she became a HR Generalist and she has been CIPD qualified since 1999. She now leads a team of HR Consultants and is an Accredited Go MAD® Coach. This is Nadine's first experience of book writing.

How Andy and Nadine met - the story behind the story

For Andy, 2 July 2001 was a pretty normal day, the first of a four-day Go MAD® Accredited Coach Programme. The training was an integral part of a worldwide cultural transformation programme being undertaken by a major financial services company. This particular course was one of several Andy had been delivering, and he was looking forward to helping others learn and apply the Go MAD® process for the benefit of themselves and their organisation.

For Nadine, 2 July 2001 was slightly different. She was excited to be attending a training course as a delegate rather than in her more usual role of deliverer. Having read one of Andy's books (Go MAD - The Art of Making A Difference), she was keen to learn more and develop her skills. Besides, she had heard on the grapevine that Go MAD® training was different from other training courses.

So that's how they first met.

Two days later, as part of the training, Nadine and the eleven other delegates were given the opportunity to demonstrate their understanding of the Go MAD® process by delivering a presentation. Nadine, along with her colleague Michelle, decided to use the analogy of a bus journey to help them explain the process.

Unfortunately, Andy was observing another presentation happening simultaneously, so he did not witness firsthand the success that Nadine and Michelle enjoyed. It was, however, the topic of conversation at dinner that night, and Andy was intrigued to know more about the presentation.

He invited Nadine to share and further develop the idea with the rest of the group the following day and explained that he had been planning to write a metaphor-based Go MAD® story. Andy invited Nadine to be his co-author, on the proviso that the following day's session was as good as he believed it would be.

Nadine's mind moved quickly. 'What an opportunity! Is this too good to be true, or is it just a creative chat-up line?' She had only met Andy two days earlier! And then the first of several self-belief wobbles happened. 'I can't write. I've never written a book. It wouldn't be any good. I've got no experience!' Andy listened, smiled and advised Nadine to apply the Go MAD® process she was learning.

The next day, Andy confirmed his view that Nadine, with an injection of confidence, had great potential as a writing partner. Nadine, still unsure of her ability as a writer, though somewhat reassured by Andy's experience, hesitantly agreed to the project.

Over the next twelve months, Nadine and Andy worked on the structure of the book, planning each chapter to ensure the key learning points of the Go MAD® process were embedded within the story. (Needless to say, Nadine's confidence sky-rocketed as each section was completed.)

The story you are about to read bears very little resemblance to the story that Nadine originally told on 4 July 2001. However, it does still involve a bus journey. So, whatever journey you are travelling, whether you are young or old, this book is for you. Enjoy it and take personal responsibility for making a difference.

Acknowledgements

Thanks from Andy

Thanks to the Go MAD team for feedback and ideas, especially Umang and Graham.
Thanks to Ronne for proofreading and the occasional tweak.
Thanks to Harriett for trusting me to travel in whatever direction I desire.
Thanks to Nadine for trusting the process, being fun to work with and a talented writer. That's a win!

Thanks from Nadine

Thanks to Dawn for reading chapters and boosting my confidence with her feedback.
Thanks to Joan and Pam for the tireless support and enthusiasm they've shown me throughout.
Thanks to Gordon for his patience when I've disappeared for days on end to write.
Thanks to Andy, for coaching me through the writing process and sharing his many years of writing experience with me.

Cover design and illustrations by Trevor Howarth - Thank you.

INTRODUCTION

Teresa was late for the meeting. She glanced at the diary entry to double-check: '2 July, 2:00 p.m. - meeting with Ben'. Her watch confirmed that she was already ten minutes late. As she gathered up the papers she needed, she clipped the edge of the plastic cup that was sitting on her desk. She watched the cup fall over in slow motion, hoping she had finished the coffee in it. Of course, she knew she hadn't - she never drank the whole cup - and she grimaced as the coffee spread over the papers.

Teresa spent the next couple of minutes frantically blotting up the coffee with tissues until she was left with a wrinkled, soggy, sepia-tinted set of important papers. She peeled them apart, one by one, and decided that there wasn't time to print a new set; these would have to do.

"I hate being late for meetings with Ben," she thought as she half walked, half ran along the corridor to his office. She knew she wouldn't get a hard time; Ben wasn't like that. But he did own the business, and Teresa, along with the other members of the team, always wanted to do her best for him, including arriving on time for meetings.

Teresa paused outside Ben's office just long enough to catch her breath. Then she walked in. Ben was standing up, facing the wall behind his desk and looking closely at one of the pictures there. As he turned to Teresa and smiled his usual warm smile, she heard him say quietly, almost to himself, "That takes me back a few years."

Then, looking up, Ben asked, "How are you today, Teresa?" He gestured for her to sit down.

"I'm fine," she replied, taking her seat in the squashy leather chair.

"Just fine?" Ben questioned as he too sat down.

"Bit hectic this morning, Ben," Teresa replied, and they both laughed as she showed Ben the papers that were now beginning to curl as they dried.

"I suppose you don't want another coffee, then?" Ben joked.

"No, thank you, but some water would be nice," she replied.

Before Ben left to get the water, he asked Teresa if there was anything else on her mind. She told him about some of the things that were troubling her at the moment. She always found it easy to talk to Ben. He seemed genuinely interested in his people and would go out of his way to help in any way he could.

When he'd left, Teresa sat back and looked around Ben's office. It was furnished in much the same way as so many other offices, but there was something that made it different: Ben's pictures. Framed carefully, each one of the dozen or more was a permanent reminder of the many successes Ben had achieved over the years. Some showed him receiving awards for successful business ventures; others pictured him receiving other honours. The picture of Ben in his cap and gown receiving an honorary university degree always made Teresa smile. The most recent addition was the picture of Ben at Buckingham Palace, standing tall and proudly holding out the MBE he had just received. His wife and family were there with him, supportive as always.

Teresa's eyes moved to the picture that Ben had been looking at as she'd come in. As she stood up to take a closer look, she realised it wasn't a picture at all. For the first time she saw the rows of what appeared to be bus tickets. She guessed they were fairly old as she examined the frayed edges and yellowing paper that had been arranged neatly in the frame. She jumped when Ben came back into the room.

"That's the story of my success you're looking at there," he said.

Puzzled, she turned to look at him. "Aren't they just bus tickets, Ben?" she asked.

"They're more than tickets, Teresa," he answered. "They're the wisdom that I learnt from two people I once knew. Each ticket represents a step towards the differences I've made in my life."

Teresa turned back and peered closely at the tickets, trying to read the now faded statements written on them.

"If you're interested, we could use this meeting for me to tell you the story," Ben suggested.

"Yes, I'm definitely interested," she replied. "I might learn something for myself."

"I guarantee you will," he said. Inviting Teresa to take her seat once more, he sat down himself.

"It happened more years ago than I care to remember," Ben began, "but the story is still as vivid as if it happened last week." Ben paused briefly as the memory came flooding back to his mind. Smiling, he continued. "The Ben who took those bus journeys was a very different person to the one you know today, Teresa. He was in a rut, unhappy with so many things in his life, and he had no idea how to change. Just as he was a passenger on the bus each day, he was a passenger in his own life, being driven through it by other things and other people. Because he didn't know what he wanted, he was happy to be driven along any road, hoping it might take him somewhere he wanted to be. It rarely did."

Ben swivelled in his chair to face the tickets, and continued.

"Let me tell you the story of Ben back then and of how he changed all that - of how he made a difference."

12

2 JULY

The bus arrived on time, much the same as every other day.

The people in the queue shuffled forward, rummaging in their bags and pockets for bus passes. One or two checked the coins they were holding, making sure they had the correct fare.

As the bus came to a stop, the door opened to allow the people to board.

Ben continued to shuffle forward, waiting for his turn to step onto the bus and start another journey - the journey he made most days, at the same time and from the same bus stop.

As he walked along the aisle, Ben spotted a seat next to another passenger and made his way towards it. Sitting down, he put his bag on the floor at his feet and looked around.

In front of him again was the young man who, Ben thought, would probably look more comfortable if he was still wearing his school uniform instead of the suit he'd obviously bought for his first job. Ben tried to make out what music he was listening to but, as usual, could only hear a drumbeat and an annoying hiss. He laughed to himself. "I'm only in my early 20s and already I'm starting to think like my father," he thought.

He glanced across the aisle and saw the woman who was always too engrossed in her newspaper to notice any of the other passengers. She always sat in the same place, wearing the same hat and coat, regardless of the weather.

As the bus pulled away from the stop, Ben looked straight ahead, past the other seats, beyond the stairway to the other deck and the luggage rack opposite, and focused his attention on the road ahead.

By the time the conductor was standing next to him, Ben had drifted off with his thoughts and, although his eyes were open, he wasn't looking at anything around him.

"Good morning, sir," the conductor said politely, as he did every day.

His thoughts interrupted, Ben looked up at the conductor.

"Miles away, sir?" the conductor asked, smiling at Ben.

"Er, yes. Yes, I was. I was just thinking about things," Ben answered, beginning to drift back to his thoughts again.

"Well, don't let me stop you, sir. Town centre as usual?" Ben nodded, and the conductor handed him his ticket in exchange for Ben's fare.

The conductor walked to the front of the bus and stood chatting with the driver for a while. They glanced at Ben for a moment, then looked back at each other and nodded in obvious agreement.

As the bus pulled away from the next stop, the conductor made his way down the aisle to collect the newcomers' fares.

"If I may say so, you do look a little anxious today," the conductor remarked as he stood next to Ben once more.

Ben looked up at him. He saw past the uniform, the ticket machine and the leather money pouch, and noticed a kind, warm smile. He'd never really looked at the conductor before - not properly, anyway - and he'd certainly never spoken to him other than to thank him for his ticket each day.

Ben noticed his unruly grey hair and thought how at odds it was with the rest of him. His face was almost unlined, and he was tall and slender. Ben couldn't decide how old the conductor was, but he guessed he was younger than his hair suggested. The most striking thing that Ben noticed about the conductor was his eyes - they were icy blue and so piercing that Ben wondered if the conductor could see into his mind.

Today, for the first time, the conductor had made him realise something - that actually, he was anxious!

"I was thinking about my life - my job, my friends and family. I know I need to make changes, make differences to my life. I just don't know how to go about doing it," Ben blurted out, without stopping to think what he was saying.

"Perhaps we can be of some assistance, then," the conductor offered, indicating himself and the driver.

"Is there enough time for you to help me?" Ben asked the conductor.

"I believe there is, sir. The journey you're about to take won't be just this one trip today. It may take a number of trips for us to help you, but if you continue travelling with us, I believe we can help you to make a difference."

3 JULY

The next day, as Ben took his place in the bus queue, he realised that this day felt different. As he waited for the bus to arrive, Ben thought about the reason why.

His conversation with the conductor the day before had intrigued him. Ben knew he had to make differences to his life, but he didn't know what they were. He was finding it hard to believe that someone else, someone who didn't really know him, was going to be able to help him. Yet he felt confident that the conductor and the driver would be able to help. The conductor had spoken to him with confidence and conviction and, because of that, Ben suddenly felt excited about the journey he was about to take.

The bus arrived on time. Ben got on, found a seat and waited patiently for the conductor to get to him. He watched as he almost glided from one new passenger to the next, collecting fares in exchange for tickets.

Ben looked up and smiled as the conductor stood next to him.

"Good morning," he said, handing over his fare.

"Good morning, sir," the conductor said, smiling back at Ben.

"I've been thinking about our chat yesterday," Ben began, "and I'm really interested in how you can help me. I've been looking forward to hearing what you've got to tell me today."

"I'm not sure I'll be telling you anything, sir," the conductor replied, still smiling.

"How can you help me, then?" Ben asked, puzzled.

"You'll find, sir..." began the conductor.

"Please call me Ben," came the polite interruption.

"...You'll find, Ben, that you already have all the answers yourself. What the driver and I can do is help you to find them."

"How?" Ben asked.

"By simply asking you the right questions, we can help you to see more clearly and understand things for yourself."

Ben thought about this for a few seconds and then asked the conductor to give him some examples of 'the right questions'.

"If I asked you, 'Where are you going today?' what would your answer be?" the conductor asked Ben.

"I'd tell you I'm going to the town centre, as usual," Ben replied.

"Did you have to think about your answer? Has your answer given us any information we didn't already have?" the conductor asked.

"I didn't have to think about it at all," replied Ben. "And no, we already know that's where I'm going."

"What are your plans for today, Ben?"

Ben began to think through what he would be doing that day. He knew that when he arrived at work, he would head straight for the break room and make himself a drink to take to his desk. He knew exactly what work he would have to do - the same work he had done for the previous two and a half years. He no longer had to think about his work; he could do it just as well with his mind on something else. He thought about his colleagues, most of whom had been doing the same job even longer than Ben. He liked the people at work, but they were all in the same rut that he was in.

Ben started to answer the question, but the conductor stopped him before he spoke.

"There's no need to answer, Ben. Just tell me what it was about that question that was different."

"Well, I had to give my answer some thought, although not too much."

"And would you have given me a one-word answer?"

the conductor probed.

"Impossible," laughed Ben.

"If you could do anything today, Ben, what would you do?" the conductor asked then.

"Oh, wow, there's a question," Ben smiled. He sat thinking about all the things he could do. He was far away from work, taking a stroll along an empty beach, hearing only the sound the sea made as it tumbled towards him and then drew back, ready to race forward once more.

"What was different about that question?" the conductor enquired, interrupting his thoughts.

"Well, in a way it felt more difficult to answer. I was having to imagine what I would do, given that opportunity."

"Again, would you have given me a one-word answer?" the conductor asked.

"Definitely impossible!"

"So, the better, more detailed answers come from the questions whose answers you have to think about - the ones where you have to focus your mind or use your imagination. Questions that start by asking *What*, *How* and *Who* will give you the best answers, Ben. You'll be answering plenty of these *high-quality questions* on your journey."

As the conductor began to turn away, he asked Ben to look around the bus and consider what he could see. Ben looked to the right and saw a man who, with his chin in the palm of his hand and his elbow resting against the window ledge, looked troubled by his thoughts. Ben noticed a young woman standing up to leave, her eyes barely leaving the floor as she edged past the man she had shared her seat with. She too appeared unhappy.

"How do the other passengers see me?" Ben wondered, and as he did, he smiled, realising that he had asked himself a *high-quality question*.

The bus arrived at the town centre. As Ben stood up to leave, the conductor met him at the front of the bus.

Ben took his ticket from his pocket and, as he was about to throw it in the used ticket slot, the conductor suggested that he keep hold of it today. Puzzled, Ben looked at the ticket. At first it appeared to be an ordinary ticket, but when he turned it over he was surprised to find two statements:

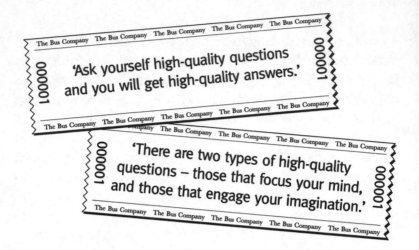

The conductor smiled and his eyes twinkled as he watched Ben's startled reaction. "Have a think about this question, Ben: *'What do you want to make a difference about?'* Have a good day. See you tomorrow."

Ben stepped down from the bus, his mind already searching for what his answer might be.

4 JULY

"What do I want to make a difference about?"

Ben had thought about little else since he'd left the conductor the previous day. So many thoughts had popped into his head, and he was beginning to feel overwhelmed by the number of ideas he was having. There were so many things he felt he wanted to do, and the longer he thought, the more extravagant the differences became. As he took his seat on the bus, he was looking forward to discussing them with the conductor.

"Hello, Ben," the conductor said as he accepted Ben's fare. "Did you answer the question I asked you yesterday?"

"I certainly did. Several times over," Ben replied. "There are so many differences I could make, I'm not really sure where to start."

"I can help you to decide, Ben," the conductor assured him. Relieved, Ben waited for him to continue.

"For you to make a difference, you need to have a strong reason why you want to do it," the conductor began. Ben's confused expression encouraged him to continue.

"Your reason why is about your motivation, your desire and passion to make the difference that you want," the conductor explained. "Your reason why will be strong if the difference you want to make is important enough to you - if it's something that you really value."

There was definitely something unusual about the conductor, Ben concluded, and it was more than just his slightly eccentric appearance. It was some sort of mesmerising quality that made Ben listen and want to share his thoughts with someone he hardly knew.

"Everything I thought of is important to me, so where do I start?" he asked.

The conductor reminded Ben of their conversation the day before.

"If you're unsure where to start, ask yourself some high-quality questions, like, *How strong is my reason why I want to make a difference?*"

"How do I know if my reason why is strong enough?" Ben asked, looking puzzled.

The conductor smiled. Ben had asked a high-quality question of his own. "It helps to use a scale, say one to ten, and to give your reason why a score," he suggested.

"How do I know if my score is high enough?" Ben asked.

"Only you will truly know if your reason why is strong

enough," the conductor answered. "Question your desire and passion for making a difference - *what might you gain or lose?"*

As he left Ben to collect more fares, he suggested that Ben continue to ask himself high-quality questions to assess his motivation.

Ben looked around the bus and noticed that there were only two passengers he'd never seen before. The others he saw most days, getting on and off the bus in the same place - the same passengers who read the same newspapers and looked out of the windows at the same scenery. He suspected that, like his, the rest of their day was predictable.

Ben began to question himself about his current situation. He thought about his friends and how some were happy with their lives and some, like himself, were not. He could think of one or two who were drifting through life, just like he was, possibly letting opportunities pass them by. He thought about his family. He loved his parents, but he felt it was time to move out of the family home he had felt safe in all his life. He thought about his father's recent retirement. Had he achieved all he had wanted to? Ben wondered if his father knew what he would do with his time now that he no longer had work to fill his days. Ben's thoughts turned to his own job and how the same things filled his time each day, starting with his journey to work.

After a short while the conductor returned to Ben's seat and asked him how he was progressing with his task.

"I was thinking about my reason for making this journey each day," Ben replied, "so I asked myself some high-quality questions about it, just to get into the swing of things. *What is important to me about making this journey? What would happen if I didn't make it every day? How important is it to me on a scale of one to ten? What's motivating me to want to make a difference?*"

The conductor nodded in agreement after each of Ben's questions.

"I realised that these questions were helping to focus my mind, so I asked similar questions about the differences I want to make," Ben continued. "I realised that many of them just aren't important enough to me right now. And that's where I came unstuck. What do I do about these things?" Ben asked.

"For now, nothing," the conductor answered bluntly. "Remember that if you are going to make a difference about something, Ben, you must have a strong reason why."

"There are things that do feel important to me," Ben said, "although I'm unclear as to exactly what I want."

The conductor turned and looked towards the front of the bus. He could see Ben's stop approaching.

"Knowing why you want to make a difference is only the first step of your journey, Ben," he said, standing aside to allow Ben to leave his seat. "Tomorrow we can talk about exactly what it is that you want. We can start to think about defining your goal."

Ben's forehead creased as his eyes widened. He was already excited about tomorrow's journey.

As he stepped down from the bus, Ben glanced at his ticket. As yesterday, the ticket was different from usual, and a message was printed on the back:

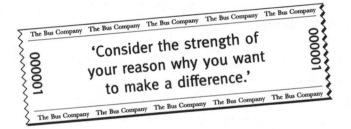

5 JULY

As Ben made his way to the bus stop he was still feeling excited by the conductor's final words from the last journey: "Tomorrow we can talk about exactly what it is that you want."

Ben had been doing some thinking since this last journey. He was beginning to identify the differences that were important to him. He wasn't yet sure exactly what they were, which was making him feel a bit confused, but he was confident that the conductor would help him to see things more clearly.

As Ben got on the bus the conductor was standing at the front, smiling and greeting passengers.

"Good morning, Ben," he said. Ben returned the friendly greeting as he passed the conductor. As he sat down in his usual seat, Ben realised that the conductor had followed him and was standing at his side.

"Perhaps it's time for you to move to a different place on the bus, Ben," the conductor suggested. Ben looked up and waited for him to continue.

"Let's move to the front of the bus today, so we can see the way ahead more clearly," he added with a knowing smile.

Ben followed the conductor to the front of the bus.

"Ben, I'd like you to meet our driver," he said.

Ben turned to look at the man who had driven the bus almost every day for as long as he could remember. The driver looked smart in his black uniform jacket. Ben noticed a long series of numbers engraved on a silver badge pinned to his lapel. Although the numbers meant nothing to the passengers, they were enough to tell them he was qualified to drive the bus. The driver had broad shoulders that looked almost too big to fit into the little cabin he sat in each day. His hair, in contrast to the conductor's, was well groomed and brushed neatly back from his face.

"Hello, Ben. It's good to meet you at last. I've been hearing lots about you from the conductor," the driver said, smiling the same warm smile as his colleague. As he returned the greeting, Ben noticed how the driver's eyes smiled at the same time, making him feel instantly at ease.

"The driver is going to help on today's journey, Ben," the conductor said as he moved down the aisle and began collecting fares.

Ben stood beside the driver's cabin. He looked out of the huge front windows at the road ahead, thinking how different the journey appeared from this view. The bus turned a corner into a tree-lined avenue. Usually, Ben saw only the bottoms of the trees from the side window, but today he noticed how their branches and leaves almost met above the middle of the avenue to form an arch. As the sun shone through the trees, the avenue became a tunnel of light beams.

"The conductor tells me you've been thinking about some differences you want to make," the driver said.

"I have," Ben replied. "Things that are important to me, although I'm not quite sure what the differences will be, and even less sure how I'll make them."

"Let's focus on the 'what' today, Ben," the driver said. "Until you have a clear picture of what you want, you can't really begin to know 'how' you're going to achieve it."

As Ben was thinking about this, the driver added, "Develop a clear, defined goal and have a strong reason why you want to succeed. Then we will focus on how to achieve that goal."

"So we'll save the 'how' for tomorrow?" Ben asked.

The driver smiled. "Maybe tomorrow, maybe the day after, but not before you know exactly what you want and why you want it."

After a short while, having digested what the driver had said so far, Ben asked him, "What makes a clearly defined goal?"

"A goal must state specifically what you want and when you want it by. And you must be able to measure when you've achieved it," the driver answered.

Ben looked confused, so the driver went on. "What do you think my goal for today is?" he asked.

"You want to complete this journey," Ben answered.

"That's more of an aim," the driver stated. "It's important to know the difference between aims and goals. Aims tend to be vague, so it's impossible to measure if you've succeeded. Ask me some high-quality questions, Ben, and use my answers to define my goal for today."

"Okay, I know your aim is to complete your journey, but *how will you know when you have completed it?*" Ben asked.

"I'll arrive at the depot," the driver replied.

"How will you know you have succeeded?" Ben continued.

"I'll arrive at the time specified in my timetable," the driver said, pointing to the laminated card leaning against the front window.

Ben reached across and picked up the timetable to take a closer look. Finding the column headed 'Bus Depot', he announced, "You need to arrive at nine-thirty. So that's your goal - to arrive at the depot at nine-thirty today."

"Can you see the difference between that goal and the aim of 'completing the journey'?" the driver asked.

"I can. It's specific, and you can measure your success easily," Ben replied, feeling quite pleased with himself.

"It helps me to see the goal written on the timetable," the driver added. "Having your goals written down will act as a reminder for you."

Ben nodded to show that he both understood and agreed with the driver.

"When defining your goal, it's important to make sure you believe it's something you can actually achieve," the driver continued. "It's pointless defining exactly what you want if you don't believe you have the experience or potential to achieve it."

Ben reflected on the driver's knowledge, skills and confidence. He noticed how effortlessly he chatted to him, yet at the same time was focused on the road and the stops he had to make. It was as if he knew exactly when he would be stopping without looking. Ben concluded that he easily had the experience to achieve his goal.

"Finally," the driver went on, "your goal should be linked to your strong reason why. It must be relevant and worthwhile."

Ben thought about what the driver's reason why was. It

was the driver's job, after all, and Ben figured that alone would be a strong reason why. But then he thought of what the driver actually did - helping people get to where they wanted to go on time - and Ben decided that too made the journey, and the goal, worthwhile.

Ben reflected on his own situation, and on how he was unsure of exactly what differences he wanted to make. He turned to the driver and asked him what he should do if he couldn't decide on a specific goal.

The driver replied, "Define a goal about a goal, and treat it as a research project. In other words, set a date by which you will have decided what your future goal will be. You don't have to define what that goal will be today."

Ben could see his stop up ahead and thanked the driver for helping him today.

"My pleasure, Ben," the driver replied. "We'll speak again soon. Before your next journey, define a goal that states by when you will know what you want."

"I will," Ben assured him.

As he turned to leave, Ben almost bumped into the conductor, who had joined them unnoticed at the front of the bus. "What," he asked Ben, "have you learned on today's journey?"

"I've learnt that defined goals state specifically what

you will achieve and by when. They should be relevant to your reason why, you need to believe you can achieve them, and you need to be able to measure your success," Ben answered. The conductor nodded in agreement.

Ben left the bus and, looking at the back of his ticket, he read these statements:

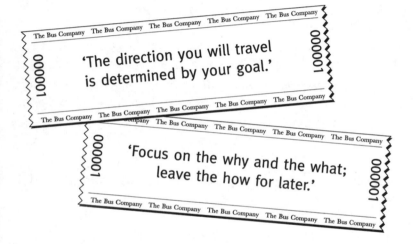

6 JULY

The first thing Ben noticed when he arrived at the bus stop was that there were no other people there. This, he thought, was strange. There were always people at the stop. He wondered if he'd missed the bus and was the first person in the queue for the next one. However, as the bus appeared in the distance, he realised this wasn't the case.

As the bus came to a halt, Ben looked around, expecting someone to come running up, looking pleased that they'd made it on time. But no one came, and as Ben climbed aboard, he realised there were no other passengers on the bus, either. The conductor and the driver were the only people he could see.

Seeing Ben's worried expression, the driver was quick to reassure him. "Relax, Ben," he said. "Today is a special journey."

"A time-travel journey, if you like," the conductor added, his blue eyes shining with excitement.

Ben felt confused and a little nervous. As if reading his mind, the conductor put a reassuring hand on Ben's shoulder.

"Today is a journey for your mind and your imagination," the driver said.

"My imagination?" asked Ben, puzzled.

"Yesterday we talked about defining your goal," the driver replied. "Visualising your success will strengthen your reason for wanting to succeed. You need to engage your imagination and create a vivid picture in your mind of what your success will look like."

"And feel like," the conductor added. "Even smell, sound and taste like, if appropriate. Using all your senses can help you to create the picture."

Ben asked the driver if he painted a picture of achieving his goal. When the driver confirmed he did, Ben asked him to 'show' him the picture. The driver's eyes widened with excitement, and he began to talk more animatedly than usual.

"I'm pulling into the depot. I check my watch and then the timetable, and I feel pleased that they read the same and I've arrived on time. I say to myself 'That's a win!' and I feel satisfied that I've helped people arrive at their destinations on time."

Ben noticed how, when the driver was talking about a 'win', he punched the air with a clenched fist.

The driver went on. "I turn the engine off and swing the cabin door open. As I stand up, I feel a tension in the muscles of my neck and shoulders. I raise my arms above my head and, clasping my hands together, I stretch up as high as I can. As soon as I drop my hands, the tension is released and I feel relaxed."

Again, Ben noticed how the driver was 'acting out' the stretching as he spoke.

"I lock the door behind me as I step down from the bus," continued the driver, "and I walk over to the depot, stretching my legs along the way. I'm sitting in the depot and drinking a cup of hot, sweet tea. I'm chatting to the other drivers, and then I go outside to get some fresh air and sunshine before my next journey." He paused slightly before he turned to Ben. "Do you see what we mean, Ben, about using your senses?" he asked.

"I do," Ben replied. "It felt like I was there with you. I noticed that you were talking as if you were actually doing it now - you certainly seemed excited enough about it." Ben paused and looked around at the empty bus. This was definitely a different journey to the one he usually travelled - certainly a more exciting journey!

The driver caught his attention once more. "Describing your goal in the present tense makes it even more specific," he explained. "If you imagine your success, it's easy to get excited about it, and once you're excited, your reason why gets even stronger."

"So once I've defined what I want, I can use my imagination to describe my future success as if it's happening today," Ben concluded.

"Yes," the driver agreed. "And once you have a vivid picture of success in your mind, and you imagine how you feel, it will strengthen your reason why."

"Another important point," the conductor put in, "is to focus on what you want, rather than what you don't want."

Ben thought about the goal he had set following yesterday's journey and decided he would state it in the present tense.

"It is two weeks from now," he began. "I have a written, clear defined goal of the difference I want to make. I feel a strong sense of achievement and am excited and confident about achieving my goal." Ben looked to the driver and the conductor for their response.

"Sounds good to me," the driver said, looking over at his colleague.

The conductor confirmed his agreement and added, "When you're defining your goal, make sure that it's something you can make happen. Daydreaming is great, so long as what you imagine yourself achieving is something whose outcome you can influence."

Ben noticed that the door had opened and other passengers were getting on the bus. He looked out of the front window and realised that he was still at his bus stop. Everything appeared to be back to normal.

The conductor leaned towards Ben and, said in a

warm, hushed tone, "If you first travel the journey in your mind, you will find it easier later to travel the journey in reality." Ben saw how his eyes sparkled and noticed an almost magical quality in them that he'd never seen before.

When the journey came to an end, the conductor handed Ben his ticket. Then he asked Ben to remember to bring his umbrella next time.

Ben looked puzzled, so the conductor explained, "There's a chance of rain, Ben, and I think your umbrella will be useful."

Ben shrugged and nodded, thanking them both as he left. His ticket read:

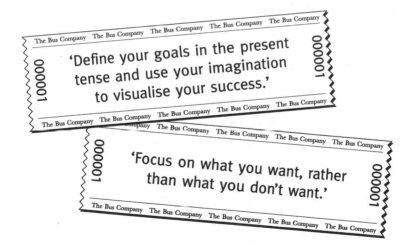

7/8 JULY

"This has been quite a week," Ben said to himself.

He was setting out for a walk, and as he began the three-kilometre circuit of his local park he reflected on all he had learned over the last five days.

He enjoyed walking at weekends, especially on days like today, when the sun was shining and he could feel its warmth on his face. This weekend was different, though. Ben reflected how, on previous weekends, he had felt as though he was walking to clear his mind, to get away from everything he knew, even for only an hour. But today, for the first time ever, he sensed he was walking towards something. And rather than clearing his mind, he filled it with the thoughts and questions the driver and conductor had planted there over the past week.

As he walked, Ben saw children playing with boats on the lake. Some of the children were floating simple pieces of wood with paper masts, no doubt lovingly constructed at home by a kind parent or grandparent, Ben thought. Others were standing at the lakeside with their friends, proudly sailing the latest in toy motorboats, manoeuvring joysticks to sail the boats faster and slower, backwards and forwards.

"They're all having the same fun, though," Ben realised. "They all have the same reason why they want to be here."

Ben heard one of the parents challenge two boys: "First one to the other side and back wins. Go!"

"They've even got defined goals," Ben smiled to himself.

As he walked past the lake, Ben saw the unused boat-house, burnt to the ground. All that was left was its skeleton, barely enough to recall the building that once stood there. Ben paused and looked at the charred remains. He remembered reading the story in the local paper. The fire had been no accident. Ben wondered if the vandals' goal had been to burn it down. If it was, they had certainly achieved what they had set out to. But he couldn't fathom what their reason why might have been.

"It's strange what drives people sometimes," he thought, realising how different things motivate different people.

Ben's walk was almost over. He'd thought about his reasons why he wanted to make a difference, and he believed his reasons were strong. He now had a goal he could work towards, and as he walked around the park he imagined how he would feel when he had achieved it - his last journey of the previous week had been the most exciting, Ben decided.

When he arrived home, he saw his umbrella in the coat stand.

"Today's weather has been so nice I'm not sure where the rain is going to come from," Ben thought. Still, he removed the umbrella from the stand and propped it up against the front door. "That way," he thought, "I will remember it tomorrow."

9 JULY

Ben's alarm rang out, and as he leaned across to switch it off, he wondered what the noise was that he could hear - a steady pattering against the window.

"It's raining," he laughed, and sure enough, when he drew back the curtains the sky was pale grey all over and the rain poured down in a relentless flow.

"I'll need my umbrella after all," he thought.

At the bus stop he noticed how everyone was standing well back from the roadside to avoid being splashed by the cars as they sped through the puddles. A young child tucked into his mum's side, taking shelter under her umbrella. One young woman, who didn't have an umbrella, was taking shelter in a shop doorway.

When the bus doors opened, Ben stepped inside and immediately turned to shake what rain he could from his umbrella to the pavement below.

"You were right about the rain," he said to the conductor, who simply smiled as he moved down the bus to collect fares.

Ben turned to the driver. "It's been so nice lately. How did he know it would rain today?" Ben asked him.

"He didn't," the driver replied. "But he did know that your umbrella would be useful."

Before Ben could ask how, the driver continued.

"Sometimes when you set out to define a goal, you begin with a vision or an aim, and these can be difficult to define and measure."

"So where does the umbrella come in?" Ben asked.

"Think of your vision or aim as your umbrella, Ben," the driver answered. The puzzled frown on Ben's face told the driver that Ben probably hadn't understood.

"Take a look at the front window, Ben," he suggested.

Ben saw the huge windscreen wiper sweeping from one side to the other, clearing the raindrops with each swipe. It moved smoothly and rhythmically from one corner of the window to the other, creating a huge arch of clear, rain-free glass. As new spots of rain fell on the window, they were immediately swept away.

"The arch or umbrella represents your vision or aim," the driver said, leaning towards the window. With his finger he drew smaller arches along the bottom of the window, then went on. "Each of these smaller arches represents a smaller umbrella, or a chunk of the bigger one. But each one is relevant to the bigger umbrella above it."

"So the smaller umbrella or chunks all add up to the bigger umbrella vision," Ben concluded.

"Exactly," the driver replied.

Encouraged, Ben continued, "And if you have defined goals for each of the small umbrellas, they add up to achieving your vision."

"That's right," the driver smiled. "Let's suppose your umbrella vision was for a happier life," he said. "You would have a number of smaller umbrellas beneath this to represent different parts of your life."

"Yes," Ben said. "I could have one for home and family, one for work, another for friends and social activities, one for health and fitness and probably one for money."

"And for each of those you would set goals which together meant you were working towards achieving your umbrella vision," the driver concluded.

"I understand now," Ben said, and as he looked out of the window he saw that the pale grey sky was white where the sun was making its presence felt. He noticed individual clouds appearing and blue sky beginning to line their edges.

"Is it looking clearer now, Ben?" the driver asked, noticing his gaze.

"It certainly is," Ben answered. To himself he thought, "Things are looking a lot clearer."

By the time Ben got off the bus, the sun had seen off most of the clouds. Only one or two were left, floating alone in the sky. Ben read his ticket:

The Bus Company

000001

'Break your umbrella vision into smaller umbrellas or chunks.'

000001

The Bus Company

The Bus Company

000001

'Have defined goals for each of these chunks.'

000001

The Bus Company

10 JULY

When Ben arrived at the bus stop he found that the queue was already quite long. The bus pulled into the stop on time and the people moved forward to get on.

He stopped to talk to the driver before taking his seat.

"Hi, Ben," the driver greeted him. "How are you today?"

"Really well," Ben replied. "I was thinking how much I'd learnt over the past few days. I now know there are differences I want to make, although I'm still not sure what they are. However, I do have a defined goal by when I will know and, importantly, a strong reason why I want to make a difference."

"It's time to start thinking about *how* you are going to get there," the driver said, as the conductor joined them at the front of the bus. Ben noticed the emphasis the driver put on the word 'how'. He remembered the message on one of his tickets from last week - 'Focus on the why and the what; leave the how for later'.

"Take a seat, Ben, and let's start thinking about what you need to do next," the conductor said, moving down the aisle to Ben's usual seat.

"The first step is to explore all the possibilities," the conductor began. "Generate as many ideas as you can about the things you could possibly do and the resources you might possibly need to help you achieve your goal."

"Possibly?" Ben queried. "That could mean anything."

"Exactly!" the conductor said excitedly. His blue eyes sparkled. "The key to a successful 'how' is to focus on the possibilities, which means, as you said, anything and everything. We can decide on definite actions later - for now it's all about coming up with as many ideas as you can."

"So where do I start?" Ben asked, eager to get going. "Ideas about what?"

"Well, there are ten really useful areas to consider, but let's start with possible resources," the conductor replied. "Take a look around the bus, Ben. *What could you possibly use to help you?*" he asked.

Ben looked around. For the first time, he noticed the adverts lining the inside of the bus, just above the windows. There were twelve in all, advertising everything from saver tickets for regular travellers, to new board games, to holidays in faraway places. He glanced out of the window and saw a bus stop across the road. There were more posters pasted to the glass, although Ben couldn't read what they were advertising.

"I could get some ideas from there," Ben suggested, pointing to the adverts.

"Possibly. *What else?*" the conductor asked,

encouraging Ben to continue.

Ben looked around and saw newspapers and books that the other passengers were reading. He pointed to a 'broadsheet' that a young man was doing battle with at the front of the bus.

"That could prove useful," Ben said, noticing that it was different from the paper he usually read during his breaks at work. He smiled as the open pages rested gently on the shoulder of the young man's companion.

The conductor smiled too. *"What else?"* he asked.

"My ticket," Ben said, remembering how useful they had been so far.

"That's great," the conductor said. "What about some of the things you could do right now? What if you went upstairs?" the conductor asked, his eyes widening as he waited for Ben's reply.

"I'd see different things, different adverts, books and newspapers," Ben replied.

"And what if you took the bus at a different time of day, or from a different stop?" the conductor challenged Ben. "What if the bus didn't turn up at all?"

"I would take a different route," Ben said. He paused and then added, "And I would see different things along the way."

"Exactly," the conductor agreed. "It's really important not to limit your possibilities to what you know now. The things you see each day, and maybe take for granted, can help you if you just look at them differently. Think about things you could do that you've never imagined you could, or would." The conductor continued, "If you only consider what you've experienced, what you believe is possible can be limited. But if you start to believe anything is possible, you'll soon be considering new things to do."

Ben nodded, but he looked a little worried. "I'm not sure I can do all of this on my own," he said, relieved to be sharing this growing concern.

"You don't need to, Ben," the conductor assured him. "This is where you can involve other people who can help you. We can talk about this tomorrow. In the meantime, remember to keep asking yourself high-quality questions."

Ben stood up to leave, pleased that he didn't have to do it all on his own. He thanked the conductor for helping him today.

As he walked away from the bus, Ben read the statements on the back of his ticket:

The Bus Company · The Bus Company · The Bus Company · The Bus Company · The Bus Company

000001

'Engage your imagination to generate ideas by asking high-quality questions.'

000001

The Bus Company · The Bus Company · The Bus Company · The Bus Company · The Bus Company

The Bus Company · The Bus Company · The Bus Company · The Bus Company · The Bus Company

000001

'Consider everything a possibility.'

000001

The Bus Company · The Bus Company · The Bus Company · The Bus Company · The Bus Company

11 JULY

Ben met the conductor at the front of the bus. He was keen to pick up where they had left off the previous day and really wanted to know how he was going to make this difference.

"I carried on thinking about possibilities last night," he told the conductor as he sat down. "I suddenly started to come up with obstacles that might stop me from achieving my goal."

"That's important, Ben," the conductor reassured him. "Now go on and ask yourself, *How could I possibly overcome these obstacles?*"

"It's a bit like developing a contingency plan in case things go wrong," Ben said.

"I guess so," the conductor agreed. "And it's important to do so, because things don't always go as planned. You should also consider, *What are the possible implications and risks in pursuing my goal?*"

"I'm even more convinced now that I can't do all this on my own," Ben said, referring to their conversation of the previous day.

"So whom could you possibly involve to help you, Ben?" the conductor challenged.

Ben thought for a while and then said, laughing, "I've

52

been involving you and the driver from the beginning."

"You certainly have," the conductor said, joining in the laughter. *"Who else could you involve?"*

Ben went on to list the members of his family, his friends, and other people he knew. He thought about his mother and father and how they had always been there for him, helping him whenever he'd needed it. He was close to his brother and sister, too. Although they had long since left home, he often spent time with them at weekends. He thought about his friends and colleagues at work and how it was likely that some of them had differences to make, too.

"What about involving people you don't know, Ben?" the conductor asked.

"Why would someone who doesn't know me want to help me?" Ben asked, genuinely puzzled.

"Start by asking, *What are the possible reasons for involving others?"* the conductor replied.

Ben considered the possibilities he had generated the day before. "They can help me with the tasks I've got to do," Ben said. "And they may have the resources I need or even the knowledge or skill to help me."

"That's right," the conductor said. "So *how could you obtain their support and get them to buy into helping you?"*

"I could explain my reasons for involving them," Ben suggested.

The conductor nodded in agreement. "Make them feel important and explain why you need their help," he added.

"I'll do it now," Ben said. "I'll talk to three people before I get off the bus today and involve them in achieving my goal."

"Great!" the conductor encouraged him. "You've set a clear, defined goal for yourself."

Ben was quite surprised by how confidently he had set a goal to speak to people on the bus. He was shy with new people and it usually took some time for him to be himself around strangers. He looked around at the other passengers and, although he was nervous, decided to speak to the man who was sitting across the aisle, engrossed in his newspaper.

Some time later the conductor returned to Ben. "Success?" he asked.

"No," Ben replied flatly, his disappointment showing on his face. "I only managed to speak to one person who was reading a newspaper I wanted to look at. He looked at me as if I was crazy and made it quite clear he didn't want to speak to me."

"Did you consider *how you could possibly communicate*

your goal, Ben?" the conductor asked. Before Ben answered, he continued, "And did you also consider how you could possibly communicate the reason why you wanted to look at the newspaper?"

Ben winced, knowing exactly where he had gone wrong.

"If he bought the paper to read on his journey, he's unlikely to give it up easily," the conductor suggested.

"So if I'd thought of that in advance, I could have asked him to let me have it when he'd finished with it, or even asked for the pages he had already read," Ben said, beginning to realise the importance of getting people's buy-in.

"You'll find, Ben," the conductor continued, "that you need to adapt your style to influence the people you want to involve. Remember, we're all different, and so we all have different goals and different reasons why."

Ben thought about how the conductor spoke to the passengers on the bus. His goal was to collect fares from them, but he approached each passenger differently. If he was speaking to a child, he crouched down and asked them what exciting things they would be doing that day. He always seemed to be laughing with them, patting the tops of their heads as he walked away. The passengers who were busy reading were asked a simple 'Where to, sir/madam?' and the conductor made the exchange of money for a ticket as quickly as possible, leaving them to catch up with the day's headlines, or continue with their book. He would sit next to the elderly passengers, chatting with them and making sure they were okay. It didn't matter who it was, the conductor was at ease with all of his passengers. Ben realised that he considered their individual goals and reasons why alongside his own.

"Involving people is crucial to your success, Ben," the conductor explained. "Our overall goal of arriving at the depot on time is only achieved by the driver involving myself and the passengers - driving the bus would be pointless without involving them."

For the remainder of the journey, Ben thought about whom he needed to involve. But now he was also thinking about their own goals and reasons why, and how he might communicate his goal to them. He decided to capture his ideas in his notebook so he could refer to them later.

The conductor joined him once more. "You now have a long list of possibilities, Ben," he said. "Start to think about which of them are the priorities, the things you need to do first."

The conductor handed Ben his ticket, which today appeared larger than normal. Ben immediately turned it over and saw that there was more written on it than on the other tickets he'd received. It read:

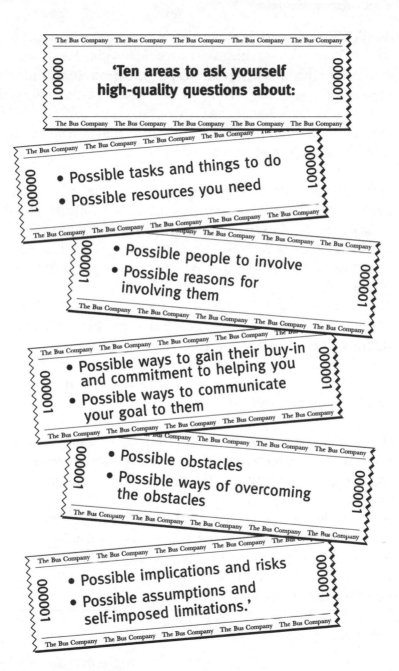

'Ten areas to ask yourself high-quality questions about:

- Possible tasks and things to do
- Possible resources you need

- Possible people to involve
- Possible reasons for involving them

- Possible ways to gain their buy-in and commitment to helping you
- Possible ways to communicate your goal to them

- Possible obstacles
- Possible ways of overcoming the obstacles

- Possible implications and risks
- Possible assumptions and self-imposed limitations.'

57

12 JULY

The driver stopped Ben as he got on the bus the next day.

"So how are you getting on with identifying your priorities, Ben?" he asked.

"I've made a start," Ben replied. "I began by asking myself, *Which actions do I need to do immediately? Which are the most important and urgent, and why?*"

"And how did you decide what is important?" the driver asked.

"I asked myself, *How important is the action to achieving my goal?*" Ben replied.

"You seem to be getting the hang of this, Ben," the driver congratulated him.

"I made good progress," Ben confirmed, "but I feel as though I've ended up with a massive list of actions - there seems to be so much to do."

"Sounds to me like you need to set some sub-goals Ben," the driver said. "Remember the umbrella goals we talked about the other day?"

Ben visualised the arc motion of the windscreen wiper blade and recalled the way the driver had broken the large vision into smaller umbrellas, using his finger to draw in the condensation. He reflected out loud, "So now I need to divide my goal into smaller pieces."

"That's right. Use my goal as an example to help you," the driver suggested.

"Your goal is to arrive at the depot on time," Ben remembered.

"So what will my sub-goals be?" the driver asked.

Ben thought for a moment and then replied, "Getting to each stop on time."

The driver agreed and added, "Every time I achieve a sub-goal I know I'm making progress towards achieving my main goal."

"That's a lot of goals to remember," Ben said, wondering how the driver managed to achieve this.

"It's important to write down your sub-goals in exactly the same way you would write down your overall goal," the driver told him, handing Ben his timetable.

Ben studied the card and noticed how detailed the information was. Along with the overall goal of when the bus should arrive at the depot, the timetable also stated what time the driver should arrive at each stop along each route that day.

"It's easier than you'd think to forget a bus stop, Ben,"

said the driver, smiling. "I've learnt from mistakes I've made in the past. Having each stop written down means that I can review my progress - I can always check if I'm on track towards achieving my overall goal."

As Ben thought about what the driver had said, he remembered how he'd often sat on the bus staring blankly at the route map posted on the side of the stairway. Along with the other passengers, he'd sat with his arms folded, unaware that he was able to review the driver's progress. He wondered if anyone would actually notice if the driver missed a stop, unless of course it was the one they wanted. He glanced down the aisle at the other passengers and concluded from their vacant stares or from the tops of their heads that they wouldn't. He turned back to the driver.

"So I can set sub-goals for each of my goals and put together a timetable of my own," Ben said.

"Yes," the driver agreed, "and you must choose when you will do those actions. Having goals is one thing, but you need to plan into your day when you're actually going to do the actions and how much time you will allocate to each priority."

"So I'll know which stop to be at by when," Ben mused.

"Before tomorrow, set yourself some sub-goals for your priorities, Ben," the driver advised, "and put together a plan showing how much time you have allocated to each sub-goal and when you will do the actions."

Ben nodded to show that he had accepted today's task from the driver. The statements on the back of his ticket read:

13 JULY

When Ben got on the bus the next day, the conductor and driver smiled and greeted him as usual, and Ben returned their greeting. Everything seemed to be as normal, but the conductor noticed that Ben seemed different. Although he had smiled at them, his eyes were sad, he looked tired and his shoulders slumped.

The conductor joined him at his seat. "Is everything okay Ben?" he asked, genuinely concerned.

"I guess if I'm honest, no, it isn't," Ben replied.

"I didn't think so. What's the problem?" the conductor probed.

"Last night I was so enthusiastic. I started to develop sub-goals and an action plan, and it was all going so well until I looked at all the things I need to do. There seems so much, and I'm not really sure I can do it," Ben said sadly, as though he had already given up.

"Would you believe me if I said that a lot of people feel this way when they think about making a difference?" the conductor asked, hoping to go some way towards reassuring Ben.

As Ben thought about what the conductor had said, he looked around at the other passengers. He remembered himself when he had first spoken to the conductor, and he saw that person in so many of them. The people who were alone, sitting rigidly with their arms folded, hoping the new passengers would walk past the other half of their seat. He doubted they really believed that they would finish the journey sitting alone. He noticed the woman who was absent-mindedly rolling her ticket into a long cone. Ben wondered if she believed she could make a difference. In fact, the only people who showed confidence were the children who would happily chat, under the watchful eye of their parents, to the passenger nearest to them.

Eventually Ben nodded, knowing that the conductor was telling him the truth.

"What you're feeling is a lack of self-belief," the conductor continued. "It's vital to believe that you can achieve the goals you've set for yourself, Ben."

"What can I do if I don't believe it?" Ben asked.

"Start by asking yourself some questions," the conductor replied. "First you need to understand why your self-belief is low, and then you need to ask, *What can I do to develop greater confidence?*"

"I started to look at what I've got to achieve," Ben replied. "I have a really strong reason why, but when I looked at the goals I've set I started to think that I couldn't do it."

"What is it about the goals that you don't believe is achievable?" the conductor asked.

"There are so many of them to achieve in such a short time," Ben replied.

"So *what can you do to increase your self-belief?*" asked the conductor.

Ben paused as he recognised a high-quality question that made him think. Almost reluctantly, he said, "I suppose I could change some of the time-scales." He paused again, reflecting on this realisation. "After all, I've set them for myself, so I can change them if I want." Ben straightened up in his seat, suddenly encouraged by this thought.

"That's right," the conductor agreed. "You can either change the time-scales or alter the measures of success to something that you believe is achievable."

"There are other goals that I'm not sure I have the skills to achieve," Ben confessed.

"Then define a goal to develop those skills," the conductor suggested, "and consider whom you will need to involve to help you."

"I guess I've started doing that by sharing the problem with you," Ben said. "I'll try and see if there is anyone else I can involve who can help me."

"You'll try?" The conductor challenged him. "Is that the most positive statement you can make?"

"I will," Ben corrected himself.

"How you talk to yourself will either help or hinder you, Ben," the conductor told him. "If you talk positively to yourself, you will increase your chances of success. Question what you say to yourself. Remember - you can be your own best friend or your worst enemy just by the messages you give yourself."

Ben realised that he needed to be more confident about his ability to make a difference. He had family and friends who he knew would help him. He'd had three jobs since he left school, all very different from each other, and so he knew he was able to learn new skills quickly.

"I'll have another think about my goals," Ben said with growing confidence. "I'll focus on ones that I don't believe I can achieve and identify the reasons. Then I can decide what I need to do to make sure I do achieve them."

"And every time you achieve a goal, celebrate a win for yourself," the conductor said. "This is good for developing confidence and keeping yourself going." Ben remembered how the driver had punched the air when he celebrated a win.

The conductor added, "There's only one person who can make this difference Ben, and that's you. You must take personal responsibility for making this difference, for making it happen."

"What do you mean?" Ben asked.

"Think about me and the driver," the conductor suggested. "The driver is responsible for making sure the passengers get to their destinations safely and on time. I'm responsible for making sure they have the correct ticket and get off at the right stop. Together, we're accountable for making it happen. We also accept responsibility if things go wrong."

"So I'm responsible for my thoughts and my actions, and one affects the other?" Ben checked, to clarify what he had just heard.

The conductor agreed, and set Ben a challenge. "Think of how you are personally responsible for making this difference, Ben."

Ben stood up to leave the bus. He was smiling and feeling so much better than when he had got on. "Thank you for helping me today," he said to the conductor.

The conductor smiled and handed Ben his ticket. The statements on the back read:

The Bus Company ... 'Your thoughts influence your actions.' ... 000001

The Bus Company ... 'Focus on talking positively to yourself.' ... 000001

14/15 JULY

That weekend Ben walked for longer than usual. It was warm and sunny, and so he set off early to make the most of the weather.

"How am I personally responsible for making the difference?" he thought.

He passed the lake and the burnt-out boat-house. For a change, he walked into the park rather than around the outside. After thirty minutes, Ben found a bench and sat down. He looked across the park, over the lush, green carpet of grass, and noticed two men playing tennis. One of them swung his racquet to hit the ball, but instead of landing on the strings, the ball hit the frame. Ben smiled to himself as it pinged off over the top of the wire fence surrounding the court.

"This racquet is hopeless!" he heard the man shout.

Ben watched as, several shots later, a similar thing occurred. Again the racquet was blamed for the mistake, and this time it was thrown to the ground.

Alongside the court a group of boys were playing football, with jumpers and bags serving as makeshift goalposts. Ben smiled, remembering how he and his friends had done the same when they were younger.

As he watched the ball weave its way across the grass, kicked from one player to the next, he thought about what it meant to be responsible for making a difference.

"Ultimately," he thought, "unless I'm prepared to take personal responsibility to make this happen, it won't. It's as simple as that."

He realised that, whilst everything he had learnt from the conductor and driver was important to his success, taking personal responsibility was at the heart of it all. He could talk about making a difference and plan for as long as it took, but unless he actually did the things he'd planned for, he wasn't going to make a difference.

Ben stood up and continued his walk through the park. He passed many people along the way but was too busy to really notice any of them. He thought about his current situation and the possible ways forward.

"I make the choices!" he stated out loud. Immediately realising what he'd done, he looked around to make sure no one had heard him. He laughed and decided that perhaps it was best to keep his thoughts silent for now.

"I've chosen to assess the strength of my reason why I want to make a difference. I've taken responsibility for that," Ben thought, feeling pleased. "Then I took responsibility for developing a clear, defined goal. I've chosen to make sure it is measurable and I've also taken responsibility for visualising my success."

He reflected on how he'd chosen whom to involve to help him, and how it was up to him whether or not he got their buy-in. He was responsible for identifying and considering possibilities, and for choosing the priorities to help him achieve his goals. He realised that if his self-belief was low, it was his choice whether to redefine his goal or work on increasing his confidence.

"It's up to me," he concluded. "I'm accountable to myself for making this difference. I make the choices."

By the time he had finished his walk and was back at the tennis court, he was feeling very pleased with himself and how he was taking his responsibility seriously. He stopped to watch the two men complete their tennis match. They were both red in the face and were moving around the court with less energy than before. When the final shot had been played they met each other at the net and shook hands. The loser was still complaining about his racquet.

As Ben walked back towards the lake, he thought about the loser blaming his racquet rather than taking personal responsibility for his own poor performance. Ben smiled as he concluded that there was no one to blame if he didn't make a difference. It was his personal responsibility - it was up to him.

16 JULY

Ben was more excited today than ever. He walked quickly to the bus stop and almost ran up the steps onto the bus.

"It's my responsibility," he almost shouted to the conductor and the driver, "and I'm taking it - responsibility, that is, for making a difference."

"Good morning, Ben," the conductor smiled. "You did well with last week's challenge, then?"

Ben took hold of the shiny silver pole as the bus moved off and began sharing his thoughts and observations from his walk in the park. The conductor and driver nodded encouragement, both clearly pleased with Ben's enthusiasm.

"So what's the next step, then?" Ben asked, looking from one to the other.

The conductor and driver exchanged a glance before the conductor replied. "There are no next steps, Ben. You've got to take action and measure the results."

"How?" Ben asked bluntly.

"Go back to your goal," the conductor answered. "After all, that's what you've got to achieve. You talked yourself about how you chose to make a difference," he continued. "As well as all the other things you're responsible for, you must choose to put time aside for monitoring your success."

"Or failure," Ben added.

"There is no failure, Ben, when you're working towards achieving your goals," the conductor told him. "There are only opportunities to learn and do things differently the next time."

"What if I fail to achieve one of my goals?" Ben asked, looking worried.

"It's always possible to change your goal," the conductor replied. "Look back at what you've done and identify the reasons for not achieving what you set out to. Was your reason why strong enough? Did you define your goal well enough?"

"Was it the right goal in the first place?" the driver added.

"And did you involve the right people and use high-quality questions to consider the ten possibility areas?" the conductor continued.

The driver and the conductor told Ben how one day the bus had broken down and so, knowing they wouldn't achieve their original goal, they set a different one. And they laughed as they went on to tell Ben about how they had to change their goal the day a pregnant passenger went into labour.

"That was definitely a good example of involving others," the conductor recalled as they described how the bus, with all the passengers still aboard, had made its way to the local hospital.

The driver rummaged in the pocket at the side of his seat and took out a picture of a newborn baby boy. He handed it to Ben. 'Thanks for helping me make my journey into the world,' the message on the back read.

"It was a win for us that day," the driver said, as Ben handed the picture back to him.

"We certainly did celebrate when we arrived at the depot that day," the conductor added. "It's really important to celebrate your success, Ben. And not just when you achieve your main goal - celebrate all the wins you have along the way."

Ben's journey was almost at an end, and not just for that day. Ben realised as he watched his stop get closer that he'd reached the end of the journey he'd taken with the driver and the conductor. They had taken him as far as they could.

"I've learnt so much from you," he said to them both. "All that's left is for me to actually make the difference."

"That's right, Ben," the conductor said.

"Everything we've helped you to learn isn't just something you use once," the driver added. "You can use it to help you make all kinds of differences all the time. Just start from the beginning."

"I will," Ben replied.

He smiled warmly at them as he stepped down from the bus for the last time as a passenger. His ticket read:

'Take action and measure the results.'

'Celebrate your wins along the way.'

Some weeks later, Ben went back to the bus stop he'd spent so many days waiting at.

He looked around and saw that he was standing with the same people he'd stood alongside so many times before. Everyone looked the same - the same vacant stares at the pavement or the road ahead; newspapers tucked under the same arms; the same coins jiggled in their palms; the young man still looking uncomfortable in his suit.

One thing, however, was very different, and that was Ben.

As the bus pulled up at the stop, Ben's excitement grew. He was looking forward to seeing the driver and the conductor again. The doors opened, and Ben waited for the other passengers to get on.

The driver and conductor looked equally pleased to see Ben, and they smiled at him as they had on each day of his journey with them.

"It's good to see you, Ben," they both said together, as if they'd rehearsed a joint welcome.

"How are things, Ben?" the conductor asked. "Been celebrating many wins?"

"I certainly have," Ben answered, "and that's the reason I'm here today. I want to thank you both for helping me, and I'd like to involve you in my celebrations."

He handed them both a small gift that he'd wrapped the night before. He shook their hands as they thanked him and took the presents from him.

"So how are you travelling these days, Ben?" the driver asked.

"That is the biggest win of all," Ben answered, and he went on to tell them about the goals he'd achieved and all he'd learnt along the way.

"I started out on this journey as a passenger - a passenger in life," he told them. "Now I'm taking responsibility for my own journeys, my own differences; I'm going to drive my own bus. I even believe I can help others to make differences, just as you helped me."

"Congratulations, Ben," the driver said. "It's great to hear that you're ready and willing to share your knowledge with others."

The conductor reached deep into one of his jacket pockets and handed Ben a small roll of paper. As he took it, Ben realised that it was a roll of bus tickets. He looked down, eagerly anticipating finding further words of wisdom on each ticket. But they were blank!

The conductor smiled as he leaned forward, tore one of the tickets from the roll and handed it to Ben.

"You can write your own tickets now, Ben," he said.

"Use these to help others on their journey."

Ben put the blank ticket, together with the roll, into his pocket. He turned and, as he left the bus, thanked both the driver and the conductor for the final time.

"That was the last time I saw the driver and conductor, Teresa," Ben said, and she could tell that although many years had passed, he remembered them as if he had seen them only yesterday.

"But what was the difference you wanted to make? What was your goal?" Teresa asked excitedly. "You never said what it was!"

Ben grinned at her enthusiasm. "Now you're starting to ask some good questions. However, you're asking the wrong person!" he said. "You need to ask yourself those questions. It's not important for you to know the details about my goals. Let's just say I wouldn't have achieved as much in my life if I hadn't discovered the process of making a difference. Now it's up to you."

As Teresa listened, she observed Ben intently - more closely than she had ever done before. She noticed his warm smile, and how his icy blue eyes twinkled as he spoke. There was definitely something that made Ben different from most other people, she concluded.

Ben paused and asked her, "So what differences do you want to make? Define your own worthwhile goals and choose your time-scale to achieve the success you want. Your journey starts here."

Teresa glanced at her watch and realised that she had another appointment with a colleague. "I've learnt so much from this last hour with you, Ben. I've definitely got some ideas of differences I need to make, and now

I feel that I know how to go about making them. Thank you," she said, as she gathered her now-dry papers together.

As she moved towards the door, Ben called after her, "Before you go..." Teresa saw him open his desk drawer and take out a small cloth bag. Ben reached inside and produced a roll of tickets - the same roll the conductor had given him.

He tore a ticket from the roll and handed it to Teresa. She looked at the yellowing ticket and recognised Ben's handwriting at once. She smiled and nodded at Ben after she'd read it. She understood now that this was the question she needed to answer.

When Teresa had left his office, Ben looked back at the tickets in the frame. He smiled to himself as he clenched his fist and said, "That's a win!"

Andy Gilbert is Group Managing Director of Go MAD Ltd, a values based consultancy firm that works around the world to help individuals and organisations make measurable differences.

To find out more about personal effectiveness and business improvement, visit the website at:

www.gomadonline.com

Or contact us at:

Go MAD Limited
Group Head Office
Pocket Gate Farm
Off Breakback Road
Woodhouse Eaves
Leicestershire
LE12 8RS
United Kingdom

Tel: +44 (0) 1509 891313
Fax: +44 (0) 1509 891582
E-mail: info@gomadonline.com